52 Br

From the publishers of *Bead&Button*, *Bead Style*, and *Art Jewelry* magazines

Fast
Fashionable
&Fun

KB
KALMBACH BOOKS

Kalmbach Books
21027 Crossroads Circle
Waukesha, Wisconsin 53186
www.Kalmbach.com/Books

Published in 2012
16 15 14 13 12   1 2 3 4 5

Manufactured in the United States of America

ISBN: 978-0-87116-713-2

The material in this book has appeared previously in *Bead Style* magazine and
the *Under $25, Gemstones, BeadStyle Around the World, 52 Bracelets, Everyday
Gemstones, Under 1 Hour, Beading Parties, Crystals,* and *Pearls* special issues.
Bead Style is registered as a trademark.

Editor: *Elisa Neckar*
Technical Editor: *Karin Van Voorhees*
Art Director: *Lisa Bergman*
Designers: *Carole Ross & Tom Ford*
Proofreader: *Erica Swanson*
Photographers: *Bill Zuback & Jim Forbes*

Library of Congress Cataloging-in-Publication Data

52 bracelets / from the publishers of Bead&Button, BeadStyle, and Art Jewelry
   magazines.

      p. : ill. (chiefly col.) ; cm.

   "Fast, fashionable & fun."
   "The material in this book has appeared previously in BeadStyle magazine and
the Under $25, Gemstones, BeadStyle Around the World, 52 Bracelets, Everyday
Gemstones, Under 1 Hour, Beading Parties, Crystals, and Pearls special issues." –T.p.
verso.
      ISBN: 978-0-87116-713-2

   1. Bracelets–Handbooks, manuals, etc. 2. Beadwork–Handbooks, manuals, etc.
3. Jewelry making–Handbooks, manuals, etc. I. Kalmbach Publishing Company. II.
Title: Fifty-two bracelets III. Title: BeadStyle Magazine.

TT860 .F542 2012
745.594/2

Contents

Basics

Cutting flexible beading wire
Decide how long you want your bracelet to be. Add 5 in. (13cm) and cut a piece of beading wire to that length.

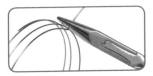

Cutting memory wire
Memory wire is hardened steel, so it will dent and ruin the jaws of most wire cutters. Use heavy-duty wire cutters or cutters specifically designed for memory wire, or bend the wire back and forth until it snaps.

Plain loop
1 Trim the wire ⅜ in. (1cm) above the top bead. Make a right-angle bend close to the bead.
2 Grab the wire's tip with roundnose pliers. Roll the wire to form a half circle.
3 Reposition the pliers in the loop and continue rolling, forming a centered circle above the bead.
4 The finished loop.

Wrapped loop
1 Make sure there is at least 1¼ in. (3.2cm) of wire above the bead. With the tip of your chainnose pliers, grasp the wire directly above the bead. Bend the wire (above the pliers) into a right angle.
2 Position the jaws of your roundnose pliers vertically in the bend.
3 Bring the wire over the pliers' top jaw.
4 Reposition the pliers' lower jaw snugly in the curved wire. Wrap the wire down and around the bottom of the pliers. This is *the first half of a wrapped loop.*
5 Grasp the loop with chainnose pliers.
6 Wrap the wire tail around the wire stem, covering the stem between the loop and the top bead. Trim the excess wrapping wire, and press the end close to the stem with chainnose or crimping pliers.

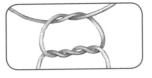

Surgeon's knot
Cross the right end over the left and go through the loop. Go through again. Cross the left end over the right and go through the loop. Pull the ends to tighten the knot.

Making a set of wraps above a top-drilled bead

1 Center a top-drilled bead on a 3-in. (7.6cm) piece of wire. Bend each end upward, crossing the wires into an X.
2 Using chainnose pliers, make a small bend in each wire to form a right angle.
3 Wrap the horizontal wire around the vertical wire as in a wrapped loop. Trim the excess wrapping wire.

Opening a jump ring or loop

1 Hold the jump ring or loop with chainnose and roundnose pliers or two pairs of chainnose pliers.
2 To open the jump ring or loop, bring one pair of pliers toward you. Reverse the steps to close.

Flattened crimp

1 Hold the crimp bead with the tip of your chainnose pliers. Squeeze the pliers firmly to flatten the crimp bead. Tug the clasp to make sure the crimp has a solid grip on the wire. If the wire slides, remove the crimp bead and repeat with a new crimp bead.
2 The flattened crimp.

Folded crimp

1 Position the crimp bead in the notch closest to the crimping pliers' handle.
2 Separate the wires and firmly squeeze the crimp bead.
3 Move the crimp bead into the notch at the pliers' tip. Squeeze the pliers, folding the bead in half at the indentation.
4 The folded crimp.

Folded crimp end

1 Glue one end of the cord and place it in a crimp end. Use chainnose pliers to fold one side of the crimp end over the cord.
2 Repeat with the second side of the crimp end and squeeze gently.

Checking the fit and finishing a bracelet

Check the fit of the bracelet against your wrist, and add or remove beads if necessary. Go back through the beads just strung and tighten the wire. Crimp the crimp beads and trim the excess wire.

Tools & Materials

Most beaded jewelry projects, including those in this book, require some combination of chainnose, roundnose, and crimping pliers, as well as diagonal wire cutters. These four tools should be your first investment when you begin beading, and should be kept close at hand as you make projects from this book. Other tools, such as the hammer, will be used only with specific projects. Use the tools as directed in the project instructions and Basics section to complete your jewelry.

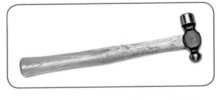

A **hammer** is used to harden and texture wire. Any hammer with a flat head will work, as long as the head is free of nicks that could mar your metal. The light ball-peen hammer shown here is one of the most commonly used hammers for jewelry making.

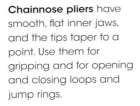

Chainnose pliers have smooth, flat inner jaws, and the tips taper to a point. Use them for gripping and for opening and closing loops and jump rings.

Roundnose pliers have smooth, tapered, conical jaws used to make loops. The closer to the tip you work, the smaller the loop will be.

A **bench block** provides a hard, smooth surface on which to hammer your pieces. An anvil is similarly hard but has different surfaces, such as a tapered horn, to help form wire into different shapes.

Crimping pliers have two grooves in their jaws that are used to fold or roll a crimp bead into a compact shape.

With **diagonal wire cutters**, use the front of the blades to make a pointed cut and the back of the blades to make a flat cut.

Metal files are used to refine and shape the edges of metal and wire surfaces.

Start with beads and findings...

Beads come in an incredible range of colors, shapes, and sizes, and can be made from a variety of materials, including crystal and glass, gemstones, pearls and shells, metals, and wood and other natural materials.

Findings like filigree components, spacers, cones, and connectors let you position and connect the elements of your jewelry, or may even serve as the main focal point.

Choose your stringing materials...

A **head pin** looks like a long, blunt sewing pin. It has a flat or decorative head on one end to keep the beads in place. Head pins come in different diameters, or gauges, and lengths ranging from 1–3 in. (2.5–7.6cm). Eye pins have a loop at one end rather than a head.

Flexible beading wire is composed of steel wires twisted together and covered with nylon.

Wire is available in a number of materials and finishes — brass, gold, gold-filled, gold-plated, fine silver, sterling silver, anodized niobium (chemically colored wire), and copper — and in varying hardnesses and shapes. Wire thickness is measured by gauge; the higher the gauge, the thinner the wire.

Cord and other fibers are alternative stringing options; ensure that the holes in your beads are large enough for the cord to pass through, as most fibers are thicker than beading wire.

Round or ribbon elastic is usually used for stretchy slip-on bracelets that must expand to fit over the wearer's hand. You may need to use a beading needle to string your beads on the elastic.

Chain is available in many finishes (sterling silver, gold-filled, base metal, plated metal) and styles (curb, figaro, long-and-short, rolo, cable). Often chain links can be opened in the same way loops and jump rings are opened.

Assemble your bracelet...

Crimp beads are small, large-holed, thin-walled metal beads designed to be flattened or crimped into a tight roll. A crimp bead cover closes over the crimp, mimicking the look of a small bead.

Crimp ends and **pinch ends** are used to connect the ends of leather, ribbons, or other fiber lacing materials to a clasp.

A **jump ring** is used to connect two components. It is a small wire circle or oval that is either cut open or soldered shut.

Clasps come in many sizes and shapes. Some of the most common are the lobster claw, which opens when you pull a tiny lever; toggle, consisting of a ring and a bar; hook-and-eye, consisting of a hook and a ring; slide, consisting of interlocking tubes; and S-hook, which links two rings.

Grab the brass ring

Brenda Schweder

Supplies
- 30–40mm round focal component
- **3–4** 12–25mm metal charms
- 7–10 in. (18–25cm) each of **6** kinds of chain in different styles and finishes, 3–9mm links
- 10–12mm 14- or 16-gauge jump ring, to accomodate the thickness of the focal component (optional)
- 7–10mm 16- or 18-gauge jump ring
- **4–6** 5mm 18-gauge jump rings
- clasp

1 Open a 7–10mm jump ring (Basics). String an end link of each of the six chains. Wrap the chains around the focal component and string a link of each chain on the jump ring. Close the jump ring and trim the excess chain.

2 Use a 5mm jump ring to attach metal charms to the 7–10mm jump ring.

3 Determine the finished length of your bracelet, subtract the diameter of the focal component, and divide that number in half. Cut two pieces of each chain to that length. Use a 5mm jump ring to attach one set of chains to the 7–10mm jump ring. Set aside the other set of chains.

4 Open a 10–12mm jump ring. Attach the remaining set of chains and the focal component. If the component has an attached loop, use a 5mm jump ring to attach the chains to the loop. String a large-hole metal accent bead on the finest chain.

5 Use a 5mm jump ring to attach the working end of each set of chains to half of the clasp. Check the fit, and trim the chains or attach an additional jump ring if necessary.

Horn bead cuff

Jane Konkel

Supplies

- **6–8** 40mm horn hairpipe beads
- **24–32** 8mm rice-shaped horn beads
- **12–16** 6mm round horn beads
- 1g 11º seed beads
- ribbon elastic
- 21–28 in. (53–71cm) 22-gauge brass wire
- G-S Hypo Cement
- big-eye beading needle (optional)

1 Cut a 3½-in. (8.9cm) piece of 22-gauge wire. Make a wrapped loop (Basics) on one end. String a 40mm hairpipe bead and make a wrapped loop. Make six to eight bead units.

2 Decide how long you want your bracelet to be, add 5 in. (13cm), and cut two pieces of ribbon elastic to that length. On each piece, string: 11º seed bead, loop of a bead unit, rice-shaped bead, 11º, 6mm bead, 11º, rice. Repeat until the strands are the finished length.

3 Tie a surgeon's knot (Basics) with both ends of the top strand. Repeat on the bottom strand. Dot the knots with glue and trim the ends.

Lush for less

Danica Losich

Supplies

- 18-in. (46cm) strand 8–12mm gemstone chips
- 8–9 in. (20–23cm) chain, 6–8mm links
- **80–100** 1½-in. (3.8cm) eye pins
- 8mm jump ring
- lobster claw clasp

1 Cut an 8–9-in. (20–23cm) piece of chain. Open a jump ring (Basics). Attach the end link of the chain and a lobster claw clasp. Close the jump ring.

2 On an eye pin, string a chip. Make a plain loop (Basics). Make 80 to 100 bead units.

3 Open one loop of a bead unit (Basics). Starting 1 in. (2.5cm) from the end of the chain without the clasp, attach the bead unit and close the loop. Attach four or five bead units to each link, leaving the link next to the clasp free of bead units.

Cosmic rings

Karla Schafer

Supplies

- 30mm crystal cosmic ring
- 20mm crystal cosmic ring
- 6mm round crystal
- 16–20 in. (41–51cm) round leather cord, 2mm diameter
- 1½-in. (3.8cm) head pin
- 2 5mm jump rings
- 5–7 7mm soldered jump rings or decorative rings
- 2 crimp ends, 3mm opening
- lobster claw clasp
- G-S Hypo Cement

1 Cut a 10-in. (25cm) piece of leather cord. Center two cosmic rings. Over both ends, string two or three soldered jump rings or decorative rings.

2 With both ends, tie an overhand knot next to the rings: Make a loop, pass the ends through it, and pull to tighten the knot. Repeat steps 1 and 2.

3 On each side, trim the ends to within 1 in. (2.5cm) of the finished length and apply glue. Place the ends in a crimp end and use chainnose pliers to gently squeeze the crimp end.

4 Open a jump ring (Basics) and attach a loop of a crimp end and a lobster claw clasp. Close the jump ring. Repeat on the other end, substituting a soldered jump ring or decorative ring for the clasp.

5 On a head pin, string a 6mm round crystal. Make the first half of a wrapped loop (Basics). Attach the soldered jump ring or decorative ring and complete the wraps.

Rings of a different color

Holly Kurzman

Supplies
- ◆ **89–116** 9–10mm 16-gauge jump rings, in colors A and B
- ◆ **2** 4–5mm jump rings
- ◆ hook-and-eye or toggle clasp

● **Tip**
To avoid scratching the surface of the jump rings, wrap masking or painter's tape around the jaws of your pliers.

1 Open half of the color A jump rings and half of the color B jump rings (Basics). Close the remaining jump rings.

2 With an open A ring, pick up a closed A ring, a closed B ring, and a closed A ring. Close the A ring. On each side of the A ring, attach a B ring.

3 Continue attaching rings in sets of three, alternating colors, until the chain is within 1 in. (2.5cm) of the finished length.

4 On each end, attach a 9–10mm jump ring, a 4–5mm jump ring, and half of a clasp.

Points & pearls

Meredith Jensen

1 On a head pin, string a pearl and make a wrapped loop (Basics). Repeat to make a total of 15 to 18 pearl units.

2 Cut a 12-in. (30cm) piece of beading wire. String three stick beads, a pearl, three pearl units, and a pearl. Repeat four or five times.

Supplies

- **15–21** 14–28mm stick beads
- **28–33** 6–8mm pearls
- **2** 8mm round pearls
- **4** 4mm spacers
- **2** 5mm bead caps
- **20–23** 1½-in. (3.8cm) head pins
- flexible beading wire, .014 or .015
- **2** crimp beads
- lobster claw clasp
- 1½ in. (3.8cm) chain for extender, 5mm links

13

3 On one end, string: spacer, 8mm round pearl, bead cap, spacer, crimp bead, lobster claw clasp. Repeat on the other end, substituting a 1½-in. (3.8cm) chain for the clasp. Check the fit and finish the bracelet (Basics).

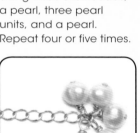

4 On a head pin, string a pearl and make the first half of a wrapped loop (Basics). Repeat to make a total of five pearl units.
5 Attach each pearl unit and the end link of chain, completing the wraps as you go.

Wired herringbone

Rebekah Gough

Supplies

- ◆ **3–4** 22–28mm gemstone nuggets
- ◆ **2–3** 10–12mm rondelles or round beads
- ◆ 48–72 in. (1.2–1.8m) 22-gauge half-hard wire
- ◆ 34–41 in. (.86–1m) 20-gauge half-hard wire
- ◆ hook-and-eye clasp

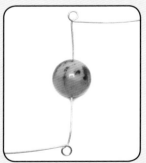

1 To make a herringbone unit: Cut a 7-in. (18cm) piece of 20-gauge wire. Center a 10–12mm bead. On each side, ½ in. (1.3cm) from the bead, make the first half of a wrapped loop (Basics).

2 Complete the wraps. Make the same number of wraps on each side of the bead.

3 Cut a 24-in. (61cm) piece of 22-gauge wire. Wrap one end around the coils twice at the base of the bead. Trim the short tail.

4 Wrap the working wire around the bead, taking it in front of and around the bottom coils once.

5 Wrap the wire around the bead, taking it in front of and around the top coils once.

6 Repeat steps 4 and 5 until you can no longer wrap. Wrap the wire twice just below the top loop. Trim the excess wire. Make two or three herringbone units.

7 To make a bead unit: Cut a 5-in. (13cm) piece of 20-gauge wire. Make the first half of a wrapped loop. String a nugget and make the first half of a wrapped loop. Make four nugget units.

8 Attach a loop of a nugget unit and half of a clasp. Complete the wraps. Attach the remaining loop and a herringbone unit. As you complete the wraps, coil the wire end over the nugget. Attach the remaining nugget units and herringbone units. Attach the remaining half of the clasp.

Mod combo

Naomi Fujimoto

Supplies

- **6–8** 16mm glass disk beads
- **10–14** 4mm bicone crystals
- 40 in. (1m) silk string, 2mm wide
- 6–8 in. (15–20cm) chain, 10–11mm links
- **6–8** 3-in. (7.6cm) head pins

1 Leaving a 3-in. (7.6cm) tail, tie a surgeon's knot (Basics) with the silk string around an end link of chain.

2 Weave the string through every other chain link. Knot the string around the end link.

3 From opposite directions, string each end through a disk bead. Pull the ends to tighten the strings. On each end, tie an overhand knot (Basics) about 1–2 in. (2.5–5cm) from the bead by making a loop, passing the end through it, and pulling to tighten. Trim the excess string.

4 On a head pin, string a bicone, a disk bead, and a bicone. Make the first half of a wrapped loop. Make five to seven disk units, and attach to links as desired, completing the wraps as you go.

● **Tip**
Use a head pin to gently push silk string through the hole of a bead.

Peridot sparkle

Patricia Bartlein

1 Cut a piece of beading wire (Basics). On the wire, center an alternating pattern of five squaredelles and four cube crystals.

Supplies

- ◆ **2** 40mm silver curved tube beads
- ◆ **5** 6mm squaredelles
- ◆ **4** 6mm cube crystals
- ◆ **2** 6mm bicone crystals
- ◆ **2** 4mm bicone crystals
- ◆ **4** 5mm flat spacers
- ◆ **4** 3mm round spacers
- ◆ flexible beading wire, .014 or .015
- ◆ **2** crimp beads
- ◆ lobster claw clasp and soldered jump ring

2 On each end, string: 6mm bicone crystal, flat spacer, curved tube bead, flat spacer, 4mm bicone crystal.

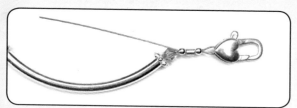

3 Attach the clasp (Basics).

Golden glow

Naomi Fujimoto

Supplies

- **2** 8-in. (20cm) strands 10–17mm beads, top drilled
- 8-in. (20cm) strand 11–13mm teardrop beads, top drilled
- **13–20** 10mm liquid gold beads
- **30–40** 6mm liquid gold beads
- **2** 4–5mm large-hole spacers
- flexible beading wire, .014 or .015
- **3** in. (7.6cm) 24-gauge wire
- **2** crimp beads
- **2** Wire Guardians
- lobster claw clasp
- 1½ in. (3.8cm) chain for extender, 8mm links

1 Cut three 13–16-in. (33–41cm) pieces of beading wire. On one wire, string a liquid gold bead and a 10–17mm bead. Repeat until the strand is within 1 in. (2.5cm) of the finished length, ending with a liquid gold bead. String a second strand.

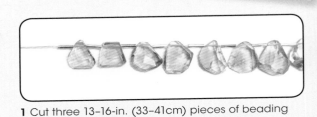

2 On the third wire, string a liquid gold bead and a teardrop. Repeat until the strand is within 1 in. of the finished length, ending with a liquid gold bead.

3 On one side, over all three wires, string a spacer, crimp bead, Wire Guardian, and lobster claw clasp. Repeat on the other side, substituting a 1½-in. (3.8cm) piece of chain for the clasp. Check the fit and finish the bracelet (Basics).

4 Cut a 3-in. (7.6cm) piece of 24-gauge wire. String a teardrop and make a set of wraps above it (Basics). Make the first half of a wrapped loop (Basics) perpendicular to the bead. Attach the end link of chain and complete the wraps.

Silky chain

Ute Bernsen

1 Cut three 5½–6½-in. (14–16.5cm) pieces of chain. Leaving a 3-in. (7.6cm) tail, weave a silk string up through the first link of each chain. Skip a link and weave down through the third link of each chain. Continue weaving the string up and down through links, skipping a link in between.

2 Leaving a 3-in. tail, weave another silk string down through the first link of each chain. Skip a link and weave up through the third link of each chain. Continue weaving the string down and up through links, skipping a link in between.

3 Trim each end of silk string to 3 in. On one end, tie a surgeon's knot (Basics) snugly against the chain links. Trim the excess string.

4 Weave the strings from the other end through the links adjacent to the knots in opposite directions.

5 On each end, string a bead and tie one or two overhand knots: Make a loop, pass the end through it, and pull to tighten. Trim the excess string.

Supplies

- **2** 10mm large-hole beads
- **2** 40–42-in. (1–1.1m) silk strings, in **2** colors
- 17–20 in. (43–51cm) rolo chain, 5–7mm links

Sweet repeat

Lea Rose Nowicki

Supplies

- **11–13** 13mm two-strand curved tube beads
- **30–34** 4mm bicone crystals:
  16–18 color A
  14–16 color B
- **4** 2mm round spacers
- flexible beading wire, .014 or .015
- **4** crimp beads
- two-strand toggle clasp

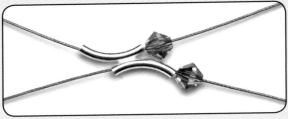

1a Cut a piece of beading wire (Basics).
b String half of a two-strand curved bead on each wire. String a color A crystal on one end of the top wire, and a color B crystal on the same end of the bottom wire.

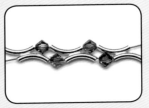

2 Repeat step 1b, alternating between color A and color B crystals, until the bracelet is within 2 in. (5cm) of the desired length. End with a curved bead.

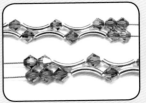

3 On one end, on the top strand, string three color A crystals. On the same end, on the bottom strand, string two color B crystals. String the patterns in reverse on the other ends.

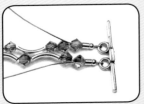

4 On each end, string a crimp bead, a spacer, and the respective loop of half of the clasp. Check the fit and finish the bracelet (Basics).

Bead bouquet

Elizabeth O'Hara

Supplies

- ◆ **5** 30mm (large) flower beads, center drilled
- ◆ **5** 14mm round beads
- ◆ **8–12** 10–20mm (small) leaf or flower beads
- ◆ 21–27 in. (53–69cm) chain, 8–12mm links
- ◆ elastic cord
- ◆ **13–17** 1½-in. (3.8cm) decorative head pins
- ◆ **5** 1½-in. (3.8cm) head pins
- ◆ **18–22** 6–7mm jump rings
- ◆ G-S Hypo Cement

1 On a decorative head pin, string a large flower bead. Make a wrapped loop (Basics). Repeat, using small leaf or flower beads. On a head pin, string a round bead. Make a plain loop (Basics). Make five large-flower units, 8–12 small leaf/flower units, and five round-bead units.

2 Cut an 18-in. (46cm) piece of elastic cord and a 21–27-in. (53–69cm) piece of chain. Fold the cord in half and string each link of the chain.

3 Tie a surgeon's knot (Basics), or square knot: Cross one end of the elastic over and under the other. Then cross the same end over and under the other. Pull both ends to tighten, apply glue to the knot and trim the excess elastic.

4 Open a jump ring (Basics) and attach a large-flower unit, two or three small-flower or leaf units, and a link of chain. Close the jump ring. Repeat, attaching the clusters about 1½ in. (3.8cm) apart.

5 Use jump rings to attach the round-bead units between the large-flower units.

Wrap up some sun

Kelsey Lawler

Supplies
- **4–6** 12mm cosmic crystals
- **15–25** 8mm round crystals, in **2** colors
- **15–25** 6mm round or bicone crystals, in **2** colors
- **8–12** 4mm bicone crystals
- **13–18** 10mm rice pearls
- **10–14** 6mm round beads
- 6–8 in. (15–20cm) chain, 3–4mm links
- 1½ in. (3.8cm) chain, 7–9mm links
- **65–100** 1½-in. (3.8cm) head pins
- **2** 4mm jump rings
- lobster claw clasp

1 On a head pin, string a cosmic crystal. Make the first half of a wrapped loop (Basics). Make: four to six cosmic crystal units, 15 to 25 8mm round crystal units, 15 to 25 6mm round or bicone crystal units, eight to 12 4mm bicone crystal units, 13 to 18 pearl units, and 10 to 14 round-bead units.

2 Attach one bead unit per link to the 3–4mm link chain, completing the wraps as you go.

3 Check the fit, and trim chain from each end if necessary. Open a jump ring (Basics) and attach one end of the chain and a lobster claw clasp. Close the jump ring. Repeat on the other end, substituting a 1½-in. (3.8cm) piece of 7–9 mm-link chain for the clasp. Attach the remaining bead unit to the extender.

Metal & pearl medley

Naomi Fujimoto

1 Cut a piece of beading wire (Basics). String pearls and bicone crystals until the strand is within 1½ in. (3.8cm) of the finished length.

Supplies
- 20–25mm metal bead
- **11–15** 10–12mm pearls
- **9–13** 4mm bicone crystals
- 15–17mm hammered ring
- flexible beading wire, .014 or .015
- 2-in. (5cm) head pin
- **2** crimp beads
- lobster claw clasp

2 On one end, string a bicone, a crimp bead, a bicone, and a lobster claw clasp. Repeat on the other end, substituting a hammered ring for the clasp. Check the fit and finish the bracelet (Basics).

3 On a head pin, string a metal bead and a bicone. Make the first half of a wrapped loop (Basics). Attach the hammered ring and complete the wraps.

Button style

Jane Konkel

Supplies

- 28mm two-hole button
- **24–28** teardrop beads, top drilled, approximately 15 x 20mm
- **5–6** 20mm vermeil beads, top drilled
- **23–31** 5mm gemstone rondelles
- **4–6** 4mm flat gold spacers
- **9** 3mm round gold spacers
- flexible beading wire, .014 or .015
- **2** crimp beads

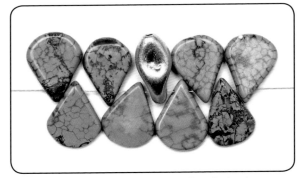

1 Cut a piece of beading wire to the desired bracelet length, plus 10½ in. (26.7cm). String four teardrop beads, a vermeil bead, and four teardrops. Center the beads on the wire.

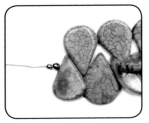

2 On each end, string a vermeil bead and four teardrops. Repeat until the strand is within 2 in. (5cm) of the finished length. Check the fit, allowing 2 in. for finishing. Add or remove beads from each end, if necessary.

3 On one end, string: 3mm round spacer, 5mm rondelle, crimp bead, two round spacers, one hole of a button, rondelle, round spacer, rondelle, second hole of the button, round spacer. Go back through the round spacer, crimp bead, rondelle, and round spacer.

4 On the other end, string a round spacer, a crimp bead, and a round spacer.

5 To make a loop for the button, string a round spacer, four rondelles, a 4mm flat spacer, and four rondelles. String a flat spacer and four rondelles, repeating until the length equals the circumference of the button. End with a round spacer.

6 Check the fit, and finish the bracelet (Basics).

Linked bracelet

Jean Yates

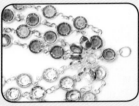

Supplies

- **3** 20mm square crystal pendants
- **113** 8mm round double-loop crystal channels:
  57 color A
  56 color B
- **8** 6–7mm jump rings
- **96** 4–5mm oval jump rings
- two-strand clasp

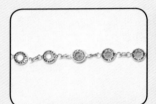

1 Open an oval jump ring (Basics) and attach two color A channels. Close the jump ring. Use jump rings to make a seven-channel chain. Make eight color A and eight color B channel chains with seven channels each.

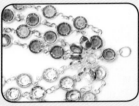

2 Use a 6–7mm jump ring to attach four color A and four color B channel chains. Use a second 6–7mm jump ring to attach the first jump ring and a single color A channel. Attach a third 6–7mm jump ring and the other loop of the single channel.

● Tip

If the single channel and jump ring from step 2 slip into the square pendants as you complete step 3, use a pin to anchor the jump ring to a piece of Styrofoam or corkboard.

3 String three square pendants over the single channel. Use a 6–7mm jump ring to attach the channel's remaining jump ring and four color A and four color B channel chains.

4 On each end, use a 6–7mm jump ring to attach the four color A channel chains and one loop of a two-strand clasp. Repeat with the color B channel chains.

Customized cuff

Rupa Balachandar

1 Use your fingers to flatten the edges of the filigree. Apply a thin coating of adhesive to the back of the filigree and to the center of the cuff. Allow to dry for 5 minutes. Press the surfaces together. Allow to dry completely.

2 Glue a 12mm flat-bottom crystal to the center of the filigree as in step 1.

3 Glue a cupped rhinestone to each of the four corners of the filigree as in step 1.

Supplies

- ◆ 55mm filigree
- ◆ 12mm flat-bottom crystal
- ◆ **4** 6mm cupped rhinestones
- ◆ 35mm gold-plated cuff
- ◆ E6000 adhesive

Subtle & classic

Jackie Boettcher

Supplies
- ◆ **5** 6mm pearls
- ◆ **5** 5–6mm bead caps
- ◆ 18–24 in. (46–61cm) bar-and-link chain, 7–10mm bars
- ◆ **5** 1-in. (2.5cm) head pins
- ◆ **2** 4–6mm jump rings
- ◆ lobster claw clasp and soldered jump ring

1 On a head pin, string a pearl and a bead cap. Using the largest part of your roundnose pliers, make a plain loop (Basics). Make five pearl units.

2 Decide how long you want your bracelet to be and cut three pieces of chain to that length. (Each chain should have an even number of bars.) Open the loop of a pearl unit (Basics) and attach it to the center link of all three chains.

3 On each side, attach a pearl unit to all three chains 1 in. (2.5cm) from the center. Repeat.

4 On one end, open a jump ring (Basics) and attach a lobster claw clasp. Close the jump ring. Repeat on the other end, substituting a soldered jump ring for the lobster claw clasp.

Lucite abloom

Naomi Fujimoto

Supplies

- ◆ **3** 20–30mm Lucite flower beads
- ◆ **22–24** 11mm Lucite round beads, side drilled
- ◆ **16–18** 8º seed beads
- ◆ flexible beading wire, .014 or .015
- ◆ **2** crimp beads
- ◆ lobster claw clasp and soldered jump ring

1 Cut a piece of beading wire (Basics). Center an 8º seed bead, a flower bead, and an 8º.

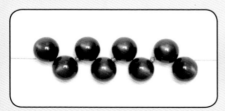

2 On each end, alternate four pairs of round beads with three 8ºs. Repeat the patterns in steps 1 and 2 until the strand is within 1 in. (2.5cm) of the finished length. End with a round.

3 On one end, string an 8º, a crimp bead, an 8º, and a lobster claw clasp. Repeat on the other end, substituting a soldered jump ring for the clasp. Check the fit, and finish the bracelet (Basics).

Crystals & links

Cathy Jakicic

Supplies

- ◆ **14–18** 4mm bicone crystals
- ◆ **7–9** 2-in. (5cm) head pins
- ◆ 13–17 in. (33–43cm) 15mm ring-linked chain
- ◆ **2** 7mm jump rings
- ◆ lobster claw clasp and soldered jump ring

1 Cut two 6–8-in. (15–20cm) pieces of chain so the rings don't line up.

2 On a head pin, string a bicone crystal, a link between two 15mm rings on a chain, and a bicone. Make the first half of a wrapped loop (Basics).

3a Attach the loop to the corresponding 15mm ring on the other chain. Complete the wraps.
b Repeat steps 2 and 3a until you've attached all the 15mm rings except the end rings.

4 On one end, open a jump ring (Basics) and attach the chains and a lobster claw clasp. Close the jump ring. Repeat on the other end, substituting a soldered jump ring for the clasp.

Batik bead bracelet

Jane Konkel

Supplies

- 17mm bone disk bead
- 14 x 30mm rectangular batik bead
- **30–45** 5mm bone spacers
- flexible beading wire, .014 or .015
- 15 in. (38cm) 2.5mm rubber tubing
- **2** crimp beads

1 Cut three pieces of beading wire (Basics). Cut pieces of rubber tubing to the following lengths: one 2½ in. (6.4cm), one 1½ in. (3.8cm), four 1 in. (2.5cm), two ¾ in. (1.9cm), nine ½ in. (1.3cm), one ¼ in. (6mm).

2a On one wire, center: 1-in. tube, spacer, rectangle bead, spacer, 1-in. tube.
b On each end, string a spacer and a ¾-in. tube.

3 On another wire, center: 1-in. tube, spacer, 2½-in. tube, spacer, 1-in. tube.

4 On the remaining wire, string a ½-in. tube and a spacer. Repeat seven times, then string a ½-in. tube.

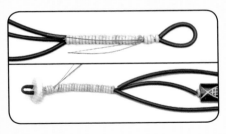

5 On one side, over all three wires, string a crimp bead, a spacer, and a 1½-in. tube. Go back through the last few beads strung. On the other side, over all three wires, string a crimp bead, a spacer, a disk bead, and a ¼-in. tube. Check the fit and finish the bracelet (Basics).

Balanced drape

Lauren Hadley

Supplies

- ◆ **2** 8–9mm beads
- ◆ **6 in.** (15cm) 24-gauge half-hard wire
- ◆ **10–12 in.** (25–30cm) cable chain, 5–6mm links
- ◆ **2** five-to-one chandelier components
- ◆ **12** 4mm jump rings
- ◆ **toggle clasp**

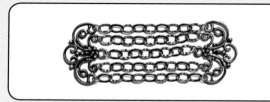

1 Cut five 1¼–1¾ (3.2–4.4cm) pieces of chain. Open a jump ring (Basics). Attach a chain and a loop of a five-to-one component and close the jump ring. Use a jump ring to attach each end of each chain and the corresponding loop of the component.

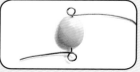

2 Cut a 3-in. (7.6cm) piece of wire. Make the first half of a wrapped loop (Basics). String an 8–9mm bead and make the first half of a wrapped loop. Make two bead units.

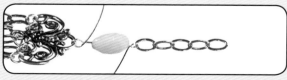

3 Cut two 1–1½-in. (2.5–3.8cm) pieces of chain. Attach the remaining loop of a five-to-one connector and a chain to respective loops of a bead unit and complete the wraps. Repeat on the other end.

4 Check the fit and trim chain if necessary. On each end, use a jump ring to attach half of a clasp and the chain.

Bubbles & waves

Jill Lindl

1 Cut three pieces of beading wire (Basics). Over all three wires, string a 9mm seashell bead. On one wire, string: bicone crystal, 6º seed bead, pearl, 6º, bicone. On each of the remaining wires, string: seven color A 11º seed beads, one color B 11º, three color C 11ºs, one color B 11º, seven color A 11ºs.

2 Repeat the pattern in step 1, alternating 9mm and 13mm seashell beads, until the strands are within 1½ in. (3.8cm) of the finished length.

3 On each end, over all three wires, string a 6º, a crimp bead, and half of a clasp. Check the fit and finish the bracelet (Basics).

Supplies

- **2–3** 13mm pewter seashell beads
- **3–4** 9mm pewter seashell beads
- **4–6** 9mm round pearls
- **8–12** 4mm bicone crystals
- **10–14** 6º seed beads
- 11º seed beads:
  2g color A
  1g color B
  1g color C
- flexible beading wire, .014 or .015
- **2** crimp beads
- toggle clasp

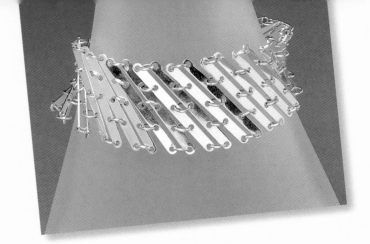

Raising the bar

Jessah Tiemens

Supplies
- **28–32** spacer bars with five holes
- **70–80** 5mm jump rings
- **2** 4mm oval jump rings
- toggle clasp

1 Open a jump ring (Basics). Attach the first holes of two spacer bars. Close the jump ring. Use jump rings to attach the third and fifth holes.

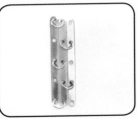

2 Use jump rings to attach the second and fourth holes of the second spacer bar and a third spacer bar.

3 Continue using jump rings to attach spacer bars as in steps 1 and 2 until your bracelet is within 2 in. (5cm) of the finished length.

4 Use an oval jump ring to attach half of a toggle clasp to the first hole of a spacer bar on one end. On the other end, use an oval jump ring to attach the other half of the clasp and the fifth hole of a spacer bar.

Chrysoprase cuff

Naomi Fujimoto

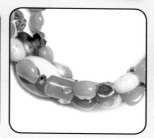

1 Cut a piece of memory wire about six coils long (Basics). Use roundnose pliers to make a loop on one end.

2 String nuggets, interspersing accent beads and faceted rondelles, until the bracelet is the finished length.

3 Make a loop and trim the excess wire.

Supplies

- ◆ **35–45** 7–18mm gemstone accent beads
- ◆ **2** 16-in. (41cm) strands 7–12mm gemstone nuggets
- ◆ **15–20** 6–12mm metal accent beads
- ◆ **15–20** 4mm faceted rondelles
- ◆ memory wire, bracelet diameter
- ◆ heavy-duty wire cutters

Heavy metals

Jane Konkel

Supplies

- **7–11** 13mm graphic feldspar nuggets
- **4–6** 12mm faceted pyrite nuggets
- 1g 8º seed beads
- 6½–8 in. (16.5–20cm) chain, 22mm links
- **2** crimp beads
- **2** crimp covers (optional)
- large lobster claw clasp
- 15mm jump ring (optional)
- **2** pairs of heavy-duty pliers

● **Tip**

Rather than trying to cut thick chain to the correct length, use two pairs of heavy-duty pliers to open and close unsoldered chain links as if they were jump rings.

1 Cut a piece of beading wire (Basics). String an alternating pattern of four 8º seed beads and three feldspar nuggets, and center.

On each end, string: pyrite nugget, 8º, feldspar, 8º, feldspar, 8º, repeating until the strand is within 2 in. (5cm) of the finished length. End with an 8º.

Cut a 6½–8-in. (16.5–20cm) piece of chain. On each end of the wire, string a crimp bead, 11 8ºs, and a link of chain one to four links from the chain's end (depending on the amount of chain you want available as an extender). Go back through the first 8º, the crimp bead, and a few more beads. Tighten the wire, crimp the crimp bead (Basics), and trim the excess wire. If desired, close a crimp cover over the crimp.

2 Check the fit and trim chain from each end if necessary. On one end, open a link of chain and attach a lobster claw clasp. Close the link. Or, use a 15mm jump ring to attach the clasp.

Bangle & dangles

Naomi Fujimoto

Supplies
- **32** 6–12mm beads
- **16**-loop bangle bracelet
- **32** 1½-in. (3.8cm) head pins

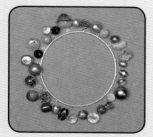

1 On your work space, arrange pairs of beads next to each loop of a bangle. Put different colors, shapes, and textures together.

2 On a head pin, string a bead. Make the first half of a wrapped loop (Basics). Make 32 bead units.

3 Attach a pair of bead units to a loop of the bangle. Complete the wraps.

4 Attach the remaining pairs of bead units to the bangle loops.

● **Tip**

This bracelet uses pairs of beads. For a fuller bracelet, you can attach three or four beads to each bangle loop, or for a minimalist look, attach just one dangle per loop.

Dazzling style

Patricia Bartlein

Supplies
- **7-8** 12mm square crystal buttons
- **3** 6mm bicone crystals
- **3** 4mm bicone crystals
- **3** 1½-in. (3.8cm) 22-gauge head pins
- **41-46** 7mm decorative jump rings
- toggle clasp

1 Open a jump ring (Basics). Attach three jump rings and one hole of a crystal button. Close the jump ring.

2a Use a jump ring to attach the set of three jump rings and one hole of another button.
b Repeat steps 1 and 2a until the bracelet is within 1 in. (2.5cm) of the finished length, ending with three jump rings on each end. Check the fit, and add or remove jump rings or buttons if necessary.

3 On each end, use a jump ring to attach half of a clasp.

4 On a head pin, string a 4mm bicone crystal, a 6mm bicone crystal, and a 4mm bicone. Make a plain loop (Basics). Make a one-bicone unit and a two-bicone unit.

5 Use a jump ring to attach the three bicone units and an end jump ring.

Disks & drops

Lacey Scott

Supplies

- ◆ **4–5** 25mm shell disk beads
- ◆ **5–6** 11mm shell disk beads
- ◆ **9–11** 2-in. (5cm) head pins
- ◆ **5–6** 10mm jump rings
- ◆ **6** 4–5mm jump rings
- ◆ toggle clasp

1 Trim the head from a head pin and make a plain loop (Basics) on one end. String a 25mm disk bead and make a plain loop. Make four or five large-disk units. On a head pin, string an 11mm disk bead and make a plain loop. Make five or six small-disk units.

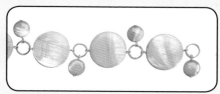

2 Open a 10mm jump ring (Basics) and attach two large-disk units. Close the jump ring. Use 10mm jump rings to attach large-disk units until the bracelet is within 1½ in. (3.8cm) of the finished length. Attach a 10mm jump ring to each end.

3 Open the loop of a small-disk unit (Basics) and attach it to a 10mm jump ring. Close the loop. Attach one small-disk unit to each 10mm jump ring.

4 On each end, attach three 4–5mm jump rings. Open the last jump ring and attach half of a clasp. Close the jump ring.

Bubbly bracelet

Naomi Fujimoto

Supplies

- **15–18** 11–13mm round Lucite beads, in assorted colors
- **7–9** 12mm round Lucite beads, in one color
- **10–13** 8–9mm round crystals and metal beads
- **15–18** 4–5mm flat spacers
- **26–32** 3mm round spacers
- oval-shaped memory wire, bracelet diameter
- **25–31** 1½-in. (3.8cm) head pins
- 4mm jump ring
- lobster claw clasp and soldered jump ring
- heavy-duty wire cutters

1 On a head pin, string a flat spacer and a round Lucite bead. Make a wrapped loop (Basics). Make 15 to 18 units.

2 On a head pin, string a round crystal. Make a wrapped loop. Repeat with a metal bead. Make 10 to 13 units.

3 Cut 1¼ coils of memory wire. Make a loop on one end.

4 String 12mm round Lucite beads until the bracelet is half the desired length.

5 String a round spacer and a bead unit. Repeat until the bracelet is within ½ in. (1.3cm) of the finished length, ending with a round spacer.

6 Trim the excess memory wire and make a loop. Open the loop (Basics) and attach a soldered jump ring.

7 On the other end, use a 4mm jump ring to attach a lobster claw clasp.

● **Tip**
Cut slightly more than one complete coil of memory wire. It's more difficult to make a loop with a stub of memory wire than it is to trim the excess later (after you've checked the fit).

Chained pearls

Cathy Jakicic

Supplies
- ◆ **8** 12mm baroque crystal pearls
- ◆ **2–3** 5mm round crystal pearls
- ◆ **3–4** 4mm round crystal pearls
- ◆ memory wire, bracelet diameter
- ◆ 5 in. (13cm) cable chain, 12mm links
- ◆ **6** 1½-in. (3.8cm) head pins
- ◆ lobster claw clasp
- ◆ heavy-duty wire cutters

1 On a head pin, string a 12mm pearl. Make a plain loop (Basics). Repeat to make a total of eight pearl units.

2 Cut a 3-in. (7.6cm) piece of memory wire (Basics). Use roundnose pliers to make a loop on one end. String a 12mm pearl, then an alternating pattern of six 4–5mm pearls and five pearl units. String a 12mm pearl. Make a loop.

3 Using two pairs of pliers to open links as you would a jump ring (Basics), separate a 2-in. (5cm) and a 3-in. piece of chain. Open an end link of each chain and attach a loop of the beaded section. Close the links.

4 Attach a lobster claw clasp and the end link of the shorter chain. Attach a pearl unit and the end link of the longer chain.

Bicone bangle

Naomi Fujimoto

Supplies

- **16** 8–15mm beads
- **2** bangles with **16** loops
- 16 in. (41cm) 20- or 22-gauge half-hard wire

1 Cut a 1-in. (2.5cm) piece of wire. Make a plain loop on one end (Basics).

2 String a loop of a bangle, a bead, and a loop of a second bangle.

3 Make a plain loop the same size as the first plain loop.

4 Attach beads to the remaining bangle loops. It's easier to anchor the bangles by attaching the first four beads at equidistant points, then filling in the rest.

● **Tip**
You can make a taller bangle by using tube beads. Or, stack additional bangles and beads. If you choose this option, make sure all bracelet loops are aligned before you start.

Briolette impact

Rupa Balachandar

Supplies

- ◆ **13** 15mm glass briolettes
- ◆ **23** 6mm bicone crystals
- ◆ 39 in. (99cm) 24-gauge half-hard wire
- ◆ 6½ in. (16.5cm) cable chain, 6mm links
- ◆ 7 in. (18cm) cable chain, 4mm links
- ◆ **23** 1½-in. (3.8cm) head pins
- ◆ **2** 7mm jump rings
- ◆ lobster claw clasp

1 Cut a 6½–7½-in. (16.5–19.1cm) piece of 6mm-link cable chain and a 7–8-in. (18–20cm) piece of 4mm-link cable chain. Open a jump ring (Basics) and attach one end of each chain and a lobster claw clasp. Close the jump ring.

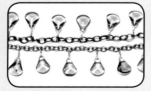

2 Use a jump ring to attach the end link of the 6mm-link chain and a link of the 4mm-link chain ½ in. (1.3cm) from the end.

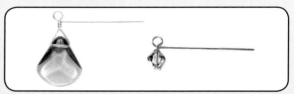

3 Cut a 3-in. (7.6cm) piece of wire. String a briolette and make a set of wraps (Basics) above it. Make the first half of a wrapped loop (Basics). Make 13 briolette units. On a head pin, string a bicone crystal. Make the first half of a wrapped loop (Basics). Make 23 bicone units.

4 Attach the briolette units to the chain as shown, completing the wraps as you go.

5 Attach three bicone units to the 4mm-link chain between the briolettes, completing the wraps as you go. Attach one bicone unit to the 6mm-link chain between the briolettes, completing the wraps as you go.

Petals & pearls

Naomi Fujimoto

1 Cut three pieces of beading wire (Basics). On one wire, center two to eight 11º seed beads. On each end, string two pearls, a bicone crystal, and two pearls. This is the inner strand.

2 On another wire, center two to eight 11ºs. On each end, string: pearl, bicone, two pearls, bicone, pearl. Repeat on the third wire. These are the outer strands.

3 On each end of the wire, string a bicone, a crimp bead, and the corresponding loop of half of a clasp. Check the fit and finish the bracelet (Basics).

4 Pin a flower over the 11ºs.

● Tips

◆ When adjusting the length of each strand, add or remove seed beads at the center of the bracelet. Though it might seem like extra work to unstring the pearls and crystals to get to them, it won't take long to restring.
◆ If you have trouble stringing .014 beading wire back through the 3mm bicones, you can finish with 3mm spacers instead.

Supplies

◆ 60–70mm fabric flower with pin back
◆ **2** 16-in. (41cm) strands 15–17mm flat teardrop pearls
◆ **16–22** 3mm bicone crystals
◆ **1g** 11º seed beads
◆ flexible beading wire, .012 or .014
◆ **6** crimp beads
◆ three-strand clasp

Lush three-strand

Naomi Fujimoto

Supplies

- **50–70** 5–12mm glass beads
- **3** 6-in. (15cm) strands three-cut 6º seed beads
- flexible beading wire, .014 or .015
- **6** crimp beads
- **6** Wire Guardians
- three-strand slide clasp

1 Cut three pieces of beading wire (Basics). On one, string 6º seed beads and glass beads until the strand is 1 in. (2.5cm) shorter than the finished length.

2 On each of the remaining wires, string 6ºs and glass beads in different arrangements until each strand is 1 in. shorter than the finished length.

3 On one end of one wire, string a 6º, a crimp bead, a Wire Guardian, and a loop of half of a clasp. Repeat on the other end. Check the fit, and add or remove beads if necessary. Go back through the beads just strung and tighten the wire.

4 Repeat step 3 on the remaining ends. Crimp the crimp beads (Basics) and trim the excess wire.

Curves ahead

Kathie Pemberton

1 Determine the finished length of your bracelet, double that measurement, and add 5 in. (13cm). Cut a piece of beading wire to that length. Center half of the clasp on the wire. Over both wires, string a 4mm round, a crimp bead, and a 5mm round.

Supplies

- ◆ **12 or more** 3 x 19mm curved tubes, silver- or gold-plated
- ◆ **7 or more** 8mm round beads
- ◆ **2** 5mm round beads
- ◆ **2** 4mm round beads
- ◆ .014 or .015 flexible beading wire
- ◆ **2** crimp beads
- ◆ toggle clasp, or lobster claw clasp and soldered jump ring

2 Make a folded crimp (Basics). String an 8mm round over both wires. Separate the wires and string a curved tube on each strand. Repeat this pattern until the strand is within 1 in. (2.5cm) of the desired length. End with an 8mm.

3 String a 5mm, a crimp bead, a 4mm, and the remaining half of the clasp. Check the fit, and finish the bracelet (Basics).

● **Tip**
To make the bracelet longer, add 2 or 3mm round spacers at the end; to shorten, eliminate a pattern of curved tubes and use an extra 4 or 5mm round bead directly after the 8mm round bead.

Get your wires in a row

Jackie Boettcher

Supplies

- **3** 9mm oval crystals
- **96–126** 4mm bicone crystals
- **6** 3mm round spacers
- **4** three-hole spacer bars, approximately 15mm
- memory wire, bracelet diameter
- **6** 1-in. (2.5cm) head pins
- heavy-duty wire cutters

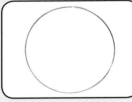

1 Cut a single coil of memory wire (Basics). Repeat twice.

2 Center an oval crystal on each wire. On each end of each wire, string a spacer, two bicone crystals, and the corresponding hole of a spacer bar.

3 On each end, string bicones to within ⅜ in. (1cm) of the finished length. String the corresponding hole of a spacer bar and make a loop.

4 On a head pin, string a bicone and make a plain loop (Basics). Make a total of six bicone units.

5 Open the loop of a bicone unit (Basics) and attach it to one of the bracelet's loops. Close the loop. Repeat with the remaining bicone units.

● **Tip**
Memory wire comes in a variety of bracelet diameters, ranging from 1¾ in. (4.4cm) to 2½ in. (6.4cm). Any variability in the size of your bracelet will come from the wire, so be sure to buy the right size to fit your wrist.

Rock band

Naomi Fujimoto

Supplies

- 16-in. (41cm) strand
  20–25mm rock crystal beads
- **9–12** 15–20mm silver nuggets
- **12** 3–4mm large-hole spacers
- flexible beading wire, .018 or .019
- 2-in. (5cm) head pin
- **2** 12–14mm soldered jump rings
- **4** 5mm jump rings
- **6** crimp beads
- lobster claw clasp
- 1½-in. (3.8cm) chain for extender, 12–14mm links

1 Cut three pieces of beading wire (Basics). On each wire, string rock crystal beads and silver nuggets until the strand is within 2 in. (5cm) of the finished length.

2 On one side, on each wire, string a spacer, a crimp bead, and a spacer. On all three wires, string a soldered jump ring. Go back through the beads just strung and tighten the wire. Crimp the crimp bead (Basics) and trim the excess wire. Repeat on the other side.

3 Open two jump rings (Basics). Attach the soldered jump ring and a lobster claw clasp to one end. Close the jump rings. Repeat on the other end, substituting a 1½-in. (3.8cm) piece of chain for the clasp.

4 On a head pin, string a silver nugget. Make the first half of a wrapped loop (Basics). Attach the end link of chain and complete the wraps.

Jump!

Beth Ruth

Supplies

- ◆ 10g 5º triangle beads
  or tiny teardrop beads
- ◆ **100–110** 5mm jump rings
- ◆ lobster claw or toggle clasp

1 Open a jump ring (Basics). Attach a 5º bead, and close the jump ring. Open a second jump ring. Attach a 5º and the previously constructed beaded jump ring unit. Close the jump ring. Continue attaching beaded jump rings to create a 1-in-1 chain until you reach the desired length.

2 Open a jump ring. Attach a 5º and the beaded jump ring unit at one end of the chain. Continue along the chain, adding a beaded jump ring to each ring in the chain.

3 Open a jump ring. Attach a lobster claw clasp to one end of the chain. Close the jump ring.

4 Open six jump rings. Attach the jump rings to each other in a 1-in-1 chain, closing jump rings as you go, and attach the chain to the other end of the bracelet to create an extender. Create six beaded jump ring units. Attach the beaded jump ring units to the end of the extender chain, and close the jump rings.

Trendy trio

Teri Bienvenue

Supplies
- **20–28** 10–15mm mother-of-pearl nuggets, in **2** colors
- **19–25** 8mm round beads
- ribbon elastic
- G-S Hypo Cement

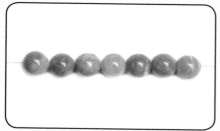

1 Decide how long you want your bracelet to be, add 3 in. (7.6cm), and cut a piece of ribbon elastic to that length. String 8mm round beads until the bracelet is the finished length.

2 Tie an overhand knot by making a loop, passing the working end through it, and pulling both ends to tighten. Glue the knot, and trim the ends. Make two more bracelets using mother-of-pearl nuggets.

● **Tips**
- ◆ If you have trouble stringing the ribbon elastic through the nuggets, fold a short piece of very fine beading wire in half to make a needle. String the elastic through the wire and pull the wire ends through the nugget.

- ◆ For variety, try complementary bead mixes or add a seed bead accent bracelet to the trio.
- ◆ You should be able to make two or three bracelets with one 16-in. (41cm) strand of beads.

Layered crystals

Naomi Fujimoto

Supplies

- **7** 38mm curved tube beads
- **12–20** 6mm crystals, in **2** or **3** shapes
- **20–30** 4mm bicone crystals
- **16–18 in. (41–46cm)** 3–5mm gemstone chips
- **10** 3mm spacers
- flexible beading wire, .012 or .013
- 1½-in. (3.8cm) head pin
- **10** crimp beads
- lobster claw clasp
- 1½ in. (3.8cm) chain for extender, 4–6mm links

1a Cut five pieces of beading wire (Basics).
b On one wire, center a curved tube bead.

2a On each end, string a chip-and-crystal pattern until the strand is within 1 in. (2.5cm) of the finished length.
b Repeat steps 1b and 2a on two other wires, stringing different chip-and-crystal patterns as desired.

3 On a fourth wire, center 2–3 in. (5–7.6cm) of a chip-and-crystal pattern. On each end, string a curved tube. Repeat on the fifth wire, stringing a different pattern.

4 On each end of each wire, string a spacer, a crimp bead, and a spacer. On one side, over all the wires, string a lobster claw clasp. On the other side, over all the wires, string a 1½-in. (3.8cm) piece of chain. Check the fit and finish the bracelet (Basics).

5 On a head pin, string a chip and a crystal. Make the first half of a wrapped loop (Basics). Attach the dangle to the end of the chain and complete the wraps.

Pretty in paisley

Rebekah Gough

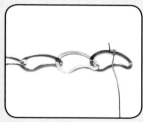

1a Cut a 7–8-in. (18–20cm) piece of chain.
b Cut a 2½-in. (6.4cm) piece of wire. Wrap the wire around one side of a link three times.

2a String a bicone crystal on the wire. Wrap the wire around the other side of the link three times. Trim the excess wire. Use chainnose pliers to flatten the wire against the link.
b Repeat steps 1b and 2a for each link.

Supplies

- **14–16** 4–6mm bicone crystals
- 35–40 in. (89–102cm) 26-gauge dead-soft wire
- 7–8 in. (18–20cm) paisley chain
- lobster claw clasp

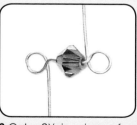

3 Cut a 2½-in. piece of wire. Make the first half of a wrapped loop (Basics). String a bicone and make the first half of a wrapped loop.

4 Attach the chain and a lobster claw clasp to respective loops of the bicone unit and complete the wraps.

Armful of chips Carol McKinney

Supplies
- **2** 15–25mm charms
- **120–180** 6–9mm gemstone chips
- **10–15** 3–4mm spacers
- memory wire, bracelet diameter
- **2** 3–4mm jump rings
- heavy-duty wire cutters

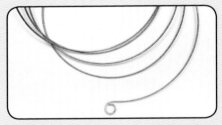

1 Cut two to four coils of memory wire (Basics). Using roundnose pliers, make a loop on one end.

2 String chips interspersed with spacers until the bracelet is the desired length.

3 Make a loop on the end. At each end, open a jump ring (Basics). Attach a charm and close the jump ring.

Creative bent

Irina Miech

Supplies

- **9** 4mm bicone crystals, color A
- **6** 4mm round or bicone crystals, color B
- **5** 4mm round crystals, color A or B
- **18** 3mm bicone crystals, color C
- **30** 3mm flat spacers
- flexible beading wire, .010 or .012
- 4 in. (10cm) 22-gauge half-hard wire
- 1 in. (2.5cm) chain, 4–5mm links
- **2** three-to-one decorative connectors
- 1½-in. (3.8cm) head pin
- **6** crimp beads
- lobster claw clasp

1 Cut a 5-in. (13cm) piece of beading wire. Center a spacer, a color A 4mm bicone, and a spacer. On each end, string: 3mm bicone, spacer, 4mm crystal, spacer, 3mm, spacer, color A bicone, spacer, 3mm. Make three crystal strands.

2 Bend a three-to-one connector so it fits around your wrist, bending slowly and carefully to achieve a smooth curve. Repeat with a second connector.

3 On each end of each strand, string a crimp bead and the corresponding loop of a connector. Go back through the last few beads strung and tighten the wires. Flatten the crimp beads (Basics) and trim the excess wire.

4a Cut a 1-in. (2.5cm) piece of wire. Make a plain loop (Basics) on one end. String a round crystal. Make a plain loop. Make four two-loop units.

b On a head pin, string a 4mm round crystal. Make a plain loop.

5 Open a loop (Basics) of a two-loop unit, attach a second two-loop unit, and close the loop. Repeat. Attach an end loop of one segment and a lobster claw clasp. Attach an end link of the 1-in. piece of chain to the remaining segment. Open the loop of the head-pin unit, attach the other end of the chain, and close the loop. Attach a two-crystal segment to the remaining loop of each connector.

Charming turn

Brenda Schweder

Supplies

- 20–25mm accent bead
- 20–25mm charm
- **12–16** 12mm tube beads
- **3** 16-in. (41cm) strands 5–9mm gemstone beads
- **12** 2–3mm round spacers
- flexible beading wire, .014 or .015

- 7 in. (18cm) 24-gauge half-hard wire
- 6mm jump ring
- 4–5mm jump ring (optional)
- **12** crimp beads
- **2** cones
- hook clasp and **2** soldered jump rings

1a Cut six pieces of beading wire (Basics). Select two pieces.
b String gemstone beads on each strand until the strand is within 3 in. (7.6cm) of the finished length.

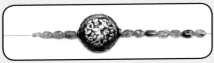

2 On the third wire, string an accent bead. Repeat step 1b on each end, making sure that the accent bead is off-center.

3 On the fourth wire, string gemstone beads, interspersing tube beads, until the strand is within 3 in. of the finished length. Repeat on the fifth and sixth wires.

4 Cut a 3½-in. (8.9cm) piece of 24-gauge wire. Make a wrapped loop (Basics) on one end. On one side, on each beading wire, string: spacer, crimp bead, the loop. Repeat on the other side. Check the fit, and finish the bracelet (Basics).

5 On each end, string a cone. Make the first half of a wrapped loop. Attach a soldered jump ring and complete the wraps. On one end, attach the hook clasp, using a 4–5mm jump ring (Basics) if necessary.

6 Use a 6mm jump ring to attach a charm and one of the soldered jump rings.

Top-speed beads

Joan Bailey

Supplies

- **16-24** 14-18mm briolettes or top-drilled beads
- **3** 5-8mm beads
- flexible beading wire, .014 or .015
- 2-in. (5cm) head pin
- **2** 5mm jump rings
- **2** crimp beads
- **2** crimp covers
- toggle clasp

1 Cut a piece of beading wire (Basics). String top-drilled beads until the strand is within 1 in. (2.5cm) of the finished length.

2 Open a jump ring (Basics) and attach the bar half of a toggle clasp. Close the jump ring. On each end, string a crimp bead and the clasp half. Check the fit, and finish the bracelet (Basics).

3 On a head pin, string three beads and make a wrapped loop (Basics).

4 Use a jump ring to attach the dangle and the bar half of the clasp.

5 Close a crimp cover over each crimp.

Colorful vacation

Naomi Fujimoto

Supplies

- **21–26** 50mm curved tube beads
- **20–25** 8mm round crystals, in **7** colors
- **2** 6mm round crystals
- memory wire, bracelet diameter
- heavy-duty wire cutters

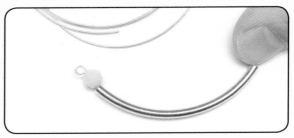

1 Determine the width of your bracelet. Select the appropriate number memory wire coils to create that width and cut the memory wire (Basics). On one end of the coils, use roundnose pliers to make a loop.

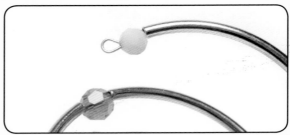

2 String a 6mm crystal and a curved tube bead. Repeat the pattern, substituting 8mm crystals for the 6mms, until the bracelet is the desired length. End with a 6mm.

3 Trim the wire to ¼ in. (6mm) and make a loop.

Easy way around

Alice Lauber

1 Decide how long you want your bracelet to be. Double that length, add 6 in. (15cm), and cut two pieces of beading wire to that length. About 3 in. (7.6cm) from one end, over both wires, string an 11º seed bead, a rondelle, and an 11º.

Supplies
- ◆ **7–9** 11mm yo-yo beads
- ◆ **4–6** 8mm crystal rondelles
- ◆ **4–6** 8mm bicone crystals
- ◆ 2g 11º seed beads
- ◆ flexible beading wire, .010 or .012
- ◆ **2** crimp beads
- ◆ lobster claw clasp
- ◆ 6mm split ring

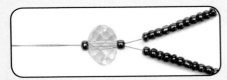

2 On each wire, string 11 11ºs.

3 Position a yo-yo bead between the wires, and make sure there are enough 11ºs to encircle it. String one wire back through the 11ºs on both wires.

4a Over both wires, string an 11º, a bicone crystal, and an 11º. Tighten the wires around the yo-yo.
b Repeat steps 2–4a until the bracelet is within 1 in. (2.5cm) of the finished length, alternating rondelles and bicones in step 4a. Also, alternate the wire end that encircles the yo-yos.

5 Check the fit, allowing 1 in. for finishing, and add or remove beads if necessary. On one side, over both wires, string a crimp bead, an 11º, and a lobster claw clasp. Check the fit, and finish the bracelet (Basics). Repeat on the other side, substituting a split ring for the clasp.

Cool curves

Donna Weeks

Supplies

- **15–21** 20–30mm curved and wavy tube beads
- 4g magatama seed beads
- **2** 4mm spacers
- flexible beading wire, .010 or .012
- **2** crimp beads
- **2** crimp covers
- toggle clasp

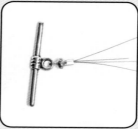

1 Cut a 20-in. (51cm) and a 12-in. (30cm) piece of beading wire (Basics). On a toggle bar, center the long wire. String one end of the short wire. Over all three ends, string a spacer and a crimp bead. With the short wire, go back through the beads just strung. Tighten the wires and make a folded crimp (Basics).

2 On each wire, string two to six magatama beads and a tube bead. Repeat until the strands are within 1 in. (2.5cm) of the finished length.

3 Over all three wires, string a crimp bead, spacer, and half of the clasp. Check the fit and finish the bracelet (Basics). Close a crimp cover over each crimp.

Peaceful blues

Tia Torhorst

Supplies
- **4–8** 8 x 12mm (medium) briolettes
- **5–9** 6 x 8mm (small) briolettes
- 1g 11° Japanese cylinder beads
- flexible beading wire, .014 or .015
- **4** crimp beads
- **4** crimp covers
- two-strand clasp

1 Cut two pieces of beading wire (Basics). On one wire, center 16 cylinder beads.

2 On each end, string a medium briolette, 16 cylinders, and a medium briolette. String cylinders until the strand is within 1 in. (2.5cm) of the desired length.

3 Center a small briolette on the second wire.

4 On each end, string 18 cylinders, a small briolette, 18 cylinders, and a small briolette. String cylinders until the strand is within 1 in. of the desired length.

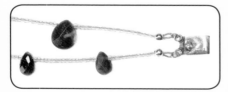

5 On each end, string a crimp bead and the corresponding loop of half of the clasp. Check the fit and finish the bracelet (Basics). Using chainnose pliers, close a crimp cover over each crimp bead.

Down to earth

Carol McKinney

1 On a bench block or anvil, hammer a marquise-shaped link. Turn the link over and hammer the other side.

2 Cut two pieces of beading wire (Basics). String 6–10mm beads until the strands are within 2½ in. (6.4cm) of the finished length.

3 On one side, over each wire, string a spacer, a crimp bead, and a Wire Guardian. Over both wires, string a lobster claw clasp. Check the fit and finish the bracelet (Basics).

4 Repeat step 3 on the other side, substituting the link for the clasp. Using the outer notch of your crimping pliers, gently close a crimp cover over each crimp.

Supplies

- 37mm marquise-shaped link
- **34-44** 6-10mm beads
- 4 3mm round spacers
- flexible beading wire, .014 or .015
- 4 crimp beads
- 4 crimp covers
- 4 Wire Guardians
- lobster claw clasp
- bench block or anvil
- hammer